Hit the Puck

Written by Emily Hooton

Collins

T0364404

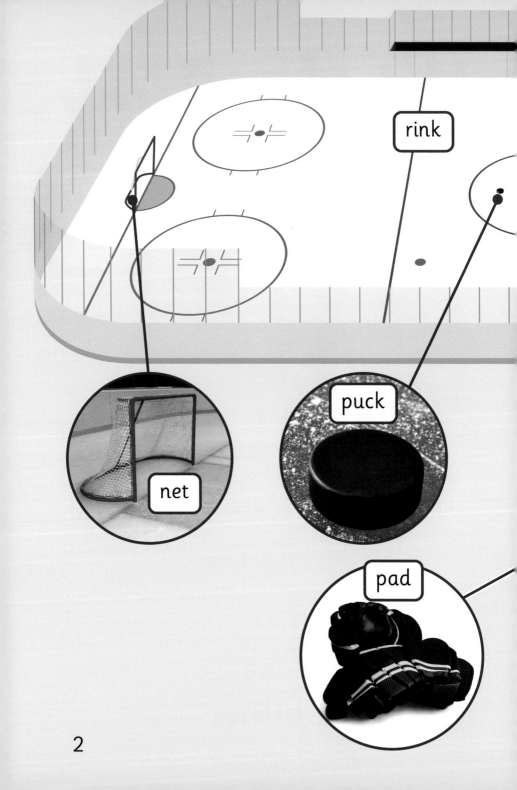

rink

net

puck

pad

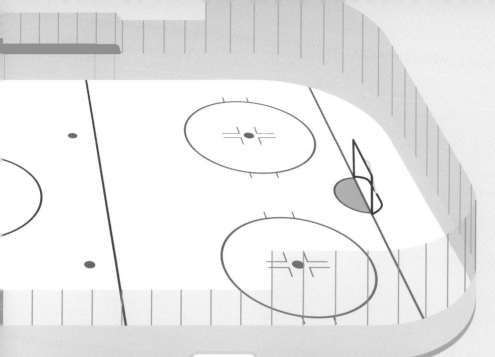

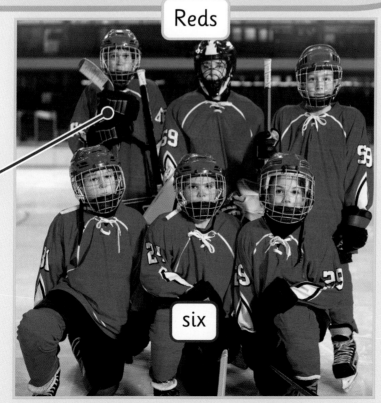

Reds

six

3

At the rink, we pull on thick kit.

The ref will toss in the puck.

7

Bang the puck. Hit it to a pal.

The puck chips up. Dash to get it back!

The puck bangs into the back of the net.

Reds get six to win the cup!

The Reds did a top job.

Hit the puck

🐾 Review: After reading 🐾

Use your assessment from hearing the children read to choose any GPCs, words or tricky words that need additional practice.

Read 1: Decoding

- Discuss the following in context. Challenge children to describe the meaning in their own words.
  - o page 6, **toss** (e.g. *chuck, throw*)
  - o page 9, **chips** (e.g. *shoots, flies*)
- Ask the children to read the following and point to the digraphs:

  rink   **thick**   **back**   **bangs**   **shot**   **dash**

- Ask the children to take it in turns to read a sentence. Challenge them to read the words aloud fluently (blending the words silently in their heads).

Read 2: Prosody

- Demonstrate reading pages 8 and 9, increasing the pace to the fastest "**Dash to get it back!**".
- Talk about why you tried to increase the pace to show the growing excitement, and speed of the players.
- Challenge children to read the pages with increasing excitement.
- Bonus content: Turn to pages 12 and 13 and encourage the children to read the newspaper as if they were a news reader.

Read 3: Comprehension

- Encourage the children to talk about the equipment used in ice hockey and what is the same or different to sports they play. For example, ask: Do you play on a rink? Do you wear pads?
- Reread page 7 and page 9. Ask: Why do you think being quick is important in this game?
- Look together at pages 14 and 15.
  - o Discuss the sequence of the pictures. Ask: What came first? What happened next?
  - o Challenge the children to retell the events as if they played the game, using, for example, "I", "we" and "us". Can they think of a sentence for each picture?